The H

istorical Mode

FASHION AND ART IN THE 1980s

Richard Martin

Harold Koda

RIZZOLI
NEW YORK

The Historical Mode has been published on the occasion of an exhibition at the Fashion Institute of Technology, New York, November 1, 1989–January 27, 1990

First published in the United States of America in 1989 by
RIZZOLI INTERNATIONAL PUBLICATIONS, INC.
300 Park Avenue South, New York, New York 10010

Library of Congress Catalog Card Number 89–62680
Hardcover ISBN 0–8478–1154–9
Paperback ISBN 0–8478–1155–7

Designed by Charles Davey
Composition by Pub-Set, Inc., Union, New Jersey
Printed and bound by Toppan Printing Company, Tokyo, Japan

Page 1: Issey Miyake. Jacket and tights in the style of a late-eighteenth-century Parisian *Incroyable*. Spring–Summer Collection, 1989. Photograph Mitsuma Fujitsuka, courtesy the designer

Frontispiece: Martine Sitbon. Shirt worn in a costume conflating early-nineteenth-century styles. Fall–Winter Collection, 1988–89. Photograph Satoshi Saikusa, courtesy *Harpers & Queen*

This page: John Galliano. Evening gown in the Directoire style. Spring–Summer Collection, 1986. Photograph Sean Cunningham, courtesy *i-D* Magazine

CONTENTS

The Historical Mode
Richard Martin and Harold Koda   7

Plates

Antiquity and Early Christian Era
2000 B.C.–A.D. 1400   17
Ancient Egypt: Giorgio di Sant'Angelo 19; **Ancient Greece:** Louis Féraud 21, Giorgio di Sant'Angelo 23, Angel Estrada 25, Douglas Ferguson 27; **Byzantine Empire:** Mary McFadden 29, Christian Lacroix 31

The Great Tradition
1400–1800   33
Late Middle Ages: Franck Joseph Bastille 35; **Late Middle Ages–Early Renaissance:** Jean-Paul Gaultier 37, 39; **Early Renaissance:** Jean-Paul Gaultier 41; **Renaissance:** Marc Bohan for Christian Dior 43, Issey Miyake 45, Maryll Lanvin for Lanvin 47; **Sixteenth Century:** Maryll Lanvin for Lanvin 49, 51; **Elizabethan Age:** Karl Lagerfeld for Chanel 53, 55, Zandra Rhodes 57; **Mid-Seventeeth Century:** Franco Moschino 59, Maryll Lanvin for Lanvin 61, Karl Lagerfeld for Chanel 63; **Early Eighteenth Century:** Elizabeth and David Emanuel 65, Karl Lagerfeld for Chanel 67, 69, 71; **Eighteenth Century:** Elizabeth and David Emanuel 73, Christian Lacroix 75, Complice 77, Guy Paulin 79; **Late Eighteenth Century:** Karl Lagerfeld for Chanel 81, Chantal Thomass 83, John Galliano 85, Issey Miyake 87

The Modern Heritage
1800–1900   89
First Empire: Romeo Gigli 91, Franco Moschino 93, Nino Cerruti for Cerruti 1881 and Martine Sitbon 95; **Early Nineteenth Century:** Hermès 97; **Mid-Nineteenth Century:** Katharine Hamnett 99; **Second Empire:** Yves Saint Laurent 101, Karl Lagerfeld for Chanel 103; **Late Nineteenth Century:** Anne Dudley-Ward 105; Christian Lacroix 107, Yohji Yamamoto 109, Anthony Price 111; **Belle Epoque:** Karl Lagerfeld for Chanel 113, Keith Varty and Alan Cleaver for Byblos 115

A Visitable Past
1900–1980   117
Turn of the Century: Hermès 119; **Early Twentieth Century:** Mitsuhiro Matsuda for Matsuda 121, Karl Lagerfeld for Chanel 123, Giorgio Armani 125, Norma Kamali 127; **c. 1918–20:** Jean-Paul Gaultier 129; **c. 1920:** Karl Lagerfeld for Chanel 131; **1923–24:** Romeo Gigli 133; **c. 1925:** Franco Moschino 135; **c. 1931–33:** Franck Joseph Bastille 137; **Early 1930s:** John Galliano 139; **1930s:** John Galliano 141; **Late 1940s:** John Galliano 143; **c. 1960:** Franco Moschino 145; **c. 1965:** Jacqueline Jacobson for Dorothée Bis 147, Carolyne Roehm 149; **c. 1969–70:** Martine Sitbon 151; **c. 1970:** Franco Moschino 153, Boy 155

Selected Bibliography   157
Acknowledgments   158
Index   159

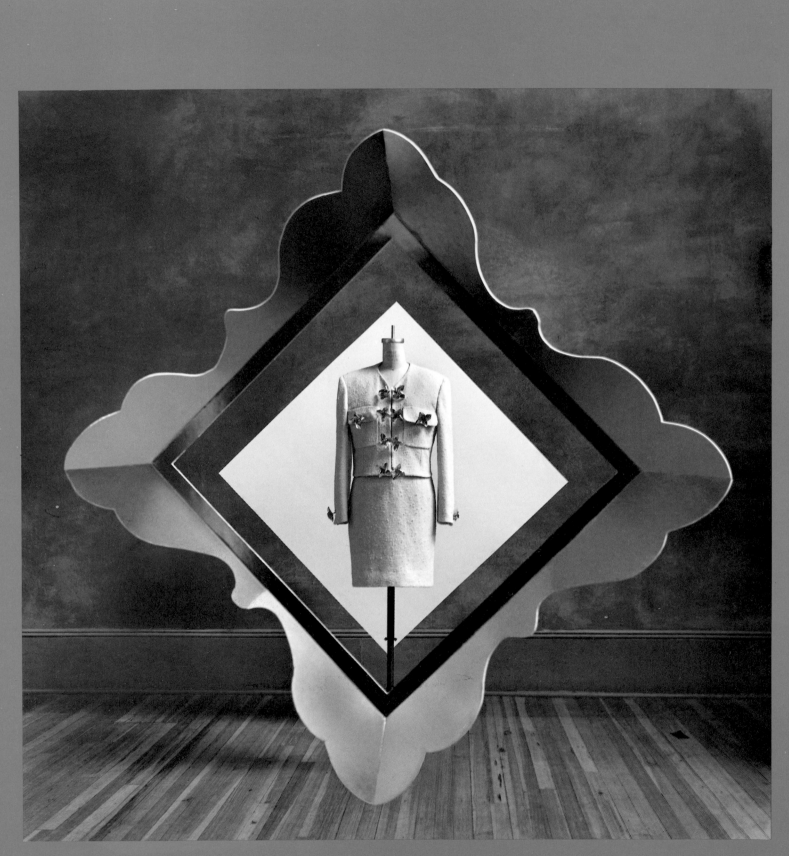

Franco Moschino. Pinwheel Suit, Spring–Summer
Collection, 1988. Photograph Josef Astor

The Historical Mode

Charles Baudelaire, it is said, once proposed that artists "use the past to confront the present." In the 1980s Baudelaire's proposition was enthusiastically embraced. Acknowledging history as an active and abiding presence in the creation of contemporary life, numerous artists and designers modeled works of art in the reconstitution, reexamination, and revelation of the past. *The Historical Mode* looks in particular at the fashion designers of the 1980s who created new art in transfiguration of the past.

Of course every era knows some appeal to history, whether in the form of symbolic revivals or a new version of a prior style. The 1980s, however, emerged as a different decade, its self-conscious and learned archaisms and renewals more fundamental than merely nostalgic. It is not that this decade created another neogothicism or neoclassicism alone. Rather, a hybrid historicism evolved, arising from a mingling of models and surpassing discrete traditions. And like the sensibility inherent in Neoclassicism of the eighteenth century, that of the 1980s has drawn the visual arts closer together, with fashion taking its place among them.

Perhaps it was in architecture among all the visual arts that the keen historical acuity of the decade was first manifest. Under the banner of "Postmodernism," with its theoretical base born in architectural criticism of the 1960s, architecture in the late 1970s moved aggressively toward the display and assimilation of historical motifs. Consorting styles leapt from the drawing boards of the previous decade and established the rhetoric of historicism for the 1980s. The decade was marked, as well, by an acute historicizing tendency in art.

This impulse to be of the past but in the present—to be in "the historical mode"—also became clearly discernible in fashion. Fashion assumed a prominent cultural role much as it had at times in the past. Such historicist appreciation enabled it to defy the triviality and caprice customarily associated with *la mode*, placing it above vanity and making it an important artistic and cultural barometer for the 1980s. Fashion's significance demanded consideration.

The decade of the 1980s was different from the preceding years of our vexing century. There was a paradigm shift, an altered mood. Overt appropriations of the historical were particularly audacious. Architect James Stirling, in his new art museum for Stuttgart, West

James Stirling and Michael Wilford. Neue Staatsgalerie, Stuttgart, 1977–84. Photograph Charles Jencks

Germany, of 1984, fused styles still identifiable with their origins but which nonetheless came together in a wholly new ensemble. Artist Barbara Bloom's references to seventeenth- and nineteenth-century art illustrated her manifestly contemporary decision to draw on historical sources, albeit selectively. In the world of fashion, designer Karl Lagerfeld created an Elizabethan figure for Chanel in 1988 but showed equal zeal in amending the Enlightenment; and designer Franco Moschino made a sendup of a 1960s Chanel suit for one collection and a Napoleonic cavalry costume for another. A Guy Paulin dress with panniers, of 1988, lifted its silhouette and textile from the eighteenth century. These garments predated our immediate past in their inspiration, but at the same time they

Barbara Bloom. *The Seven Deadly Sins: Envy*, 1988. Mixed-media construction. Courtesy Jay Gorney Modern Art, New York

extended the reach of contemporary design, not unlike the furniture of Robert Venturi, the architecture of Philip Johnson and John Burgee, or the art of Sherrie Levine. The past is not immortalized but rather resuscitated by the work of contemporary artists and designers who seize—not just touch—history and render it new.

How certain is our vision of the past? After all, we can only reconstruct a semblance of it from extant artifacts, paintings, and sculpture. The truth is that our understanding of the past is only as sure as modern scrutiny can make it. Nevertheless, the transfigured graces of ancient Rome in Charles Jencks's Colosseum chair, of 1985, and other contemporary recourses to historical episode, style, and ethos fulfill a need as powerful as any historical formula to chronicle and make peace with the past.

A retreat from Modernism accompanied the rise of historicism in the 1980s. The dauntless progressivism of the Modern movement, which posited revolution as the model for aesthetic development, is now questioned. In its place there is an enhanced appreciation of the step backward into history as perhaps the best means by which to move forward.

Few clocks are more precise than those of fashion. The resurgence of vintage clothing as a favored mode of dress for the youthful vanguard typifies the pertinence of the historical past to the 1980s. It also acknowledges the evocative and nostalgic power of garments. To examine—even exhume—history was a significant motif of popular culture of the decade. If the 1984 film *Amadeus*—which in turn inspired clothing by Jean-Paul Gaultier and other designers—was an early 1980s indication of a popular fas-

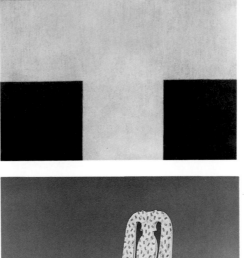

Sherrie Levine. Untitled (after Ilya Chasnik, *Suprematist Cross*, 1923), 1984. Casein on wood. Courtesy Mary Boone Gallery, New York. Photograph Zindman/Fremont

Robert Venturi for Knoll Studio. Queen Anne Chair, 1984. Machine-molded plywood. Courtesy Knoll International, New York

Charles Jencks. Colosseum Chair and Stool, 1985. Painted medium-density fiberboard and suede. Courtesy the designer. Photograph Richard Holt

Actors Glenn Close and John Malkovich in the film
Dangerous Liaisons, directed by Stephen Frears,
1988. Photograph copyright © Warner Bros., Inc.

Karl Lagerfeld for Chanel. Evening Gown with
Watteau-inspired Coat, Spring–Summer Collection,
1985. Courtesy Chanel

Antoine Watteau. *Standing Woman Seen from
Behind*, c. 1715. Etching. Bibliothèque Nationale, Paris

Antoine Watteau. *Pierrot* (called *Gilles*), c. 1718–19.
Oil on canvas. Musée du Louvre, Paris

cination with the past, then the 1986 song "Rock Me Amadeus" extended this reanimation of Wolfgang Amadeus Mozart and self-consciously recalled Chuck Berry's recording of "Roll over Beethoven" from 1956 (every decade has its flirtations with period recreations).

The 1980s were marked by a return to France of the ancien régime in new treatments on stage and screen of Choderlos Laclos's novel *Les Liaisons dangéreuses,* of 1782. In other reenactments historical conflations occurred, as in Franco Moschino's 1988–89 design of a Napoleonic cavalry costume, its origins dating from the First Empire period around 1806 but in our time created to celebrate the bicentennial of the French Revolution of 1789. A Romeo Gigli Empire dress of 1987 could as easily have been patterned after the costume of Liberty in Eugène Delacroix's *Liberty Leading the People*, of 1830, which celebrated the Empire's downfall, as the period gown of Mlle Charlotte Val d'Ognes in the 1810 painting of the same name.

In fact, the evidence of historicism in the world of fashion during the 1980s is overwhelming. British couturier John Galliano, for example, designed Empire dresses in 1986 in specific emulation of another time and place. In Paris, Karl Lagerfeld echoed eighteenth-century painting when in 1985 he created a coat for Chanel with back pleats inspired by the art of Antoine Watteau. Such journeys into the past may be prompted by specific events such as the great Watteau retrospective at the Grand Palais in Paris of 1984. They may also come about simply because designers realize that problems of apparel design may be addressed by age-old solutions. To be sure, the traditional argument against historicizing fashion is that social requirements have changed: what was appropriate to wear at Versailles, say, would be out of place in a downtown club. Bill Cunningham, fashion journalist and photographer for *The New York Times* and *Details*, has convincingly refuted these simplistic comparisons by chronicling the persistence and pertinence of traditional dress as a model for the present.

In the 1980s Lagerfeld demonstrated a mastery of varied historical sources. If the Watteau back captures the spirit of the artist's *Standing Woman Seen from Behind*, c. 1715, and his *Gersaint's Shop Sign*, c. 1720, Lagerfeld's silk suit with pants is derived from the artist's *Pierrot* (called *Gilles*), c. 1718–19. In this instance, Lagerfeld chooses a work of art that is distant, yet close. In 1985 art critic Sanford Schwartz wrote of *Pierrot* (called *Gilles*): "His face is as secretive as any by Leonardo, and there is a gravity to him that recalls Rembrandt. His blankness though, is what is fascinating. . . . He appears to know how awkward and uncomfortable he is—and, too, how his power comes from his willingness to be awkward and foolish. He is the first figure in art who, it seems, is one of us." Indeed, it may have been this "one of us" aspect that engaged Lagerfeld. Moon-faced, with pants too short, sleeves too long, gaudy pink ribbons on his slippers, and a white-flannel jacket in discord with his white-satin trousers, Watteau's Gilles could almost be thought of as a study in how not to dress—the buffoon subject for a clothing and cosmetics makeover. But in the Watteau masterpiece we see and empathize with an inner beauty and dignity more telling—even poignant—than might be evident in a more stately subject. Lagerfeld plucks Gilles from melancholy to become a modern paragon of decorum and style. He is transformed as he becomes fashion in the 1980s: yet his gravity remains and flourishes across the interval of more than 250 years.

In a series of men's jackets designed for a 1988 collection Jean-Paul Gaultier has recreated the Middle Ages in our own time. In a mixture of Victorian fantasy and the medieval, he has created a mock-heroic juxtaposition of Edward Burne-Jones and Prince Valiant as the fleur-de-lis flourishes in heraldic grandeur on the back of one coat and diamond-pattern patchwork graces the sleeves of another. Italian semiotician Umberto Eco argues, in his *Art and Beauty in the Middle Ages,* that "anyone at all who tries to interpret [medieval aesthetic theory and practice] sensitively can learn something: not because it is the expression of a civilization better than any other, but because this is the value of any civilization and any doctrine of the past, when we seek to discover its lessons for the present." Presumably prompted by reflections such as Eco's, Gaultier's knightly images step out of the International Style of the fourteenth century, joining a complex revival of the medieval spirit, one part of a broader historicist movement. For example, American architect

Edward Burne-Jones. *The Arming and Departure of the Knights of the Round Table on the Quest of the Holy Grail* (detail), c. 1890. Tapestry. Birmingham Museums and Art Gallery, Birmingham, England

Michael Graves's 1982 proposal for a Matsuya store in Tokyo features a medieval-castle facade, and crenellated towers grace a Manhattan building of 1986 by Johnson and Burgee, suggesting a medieval citadel. Scottish-American artist

Michael Graves. Model for Matsuya Department Store, the Ginza, Tokyo, 1982. Mixed media

Thomas Lawson's painting *Christminster* of 1984 literally turns an image of Wells Cathedral in England on its side. And the penumbral icons of painter Michael Abrams's *Alchemy* of 1989 have their source in the thirteenth century, though they are further inflected by fin-de-siècle Symbolism. In these endeavors we end up not with a Gothic Revival picturesque but with a Middle Ages built of notably contemporary stones. The notion that the Middle Ages were, in Eco's words, "an immense work of *bricolage*" is reinforced by the improvised and imagined Middle Ages being created in the 1980s.

The classical world, visited with such zeal by modern political and social theory, is also evoked in art and fashion. Designer Douglas Ferguson's classical wrappings in metal mesh of 1985 and

Philip Johnson and John Burgee. Office Building, 33 Maiden Lane, New York, 1986. Courtesy Park Tower Development. Photograph Nathaniel Lieberman

Michael Abrams. *Alchemy*, 1989. Oil on panel.
Courtesy Trabia-MacAfee Gallery, New York

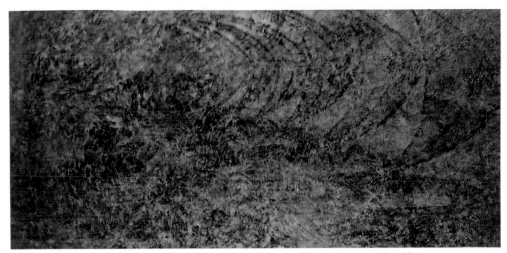

Thomas Lawson. *Christminster*, 1984. Oil on canvas. Courtesy Metro Pictures, New York

Peter Saari. Untitled, 1984. Casein and plaster on
board. Collection Fairmont Hotel, Chicago.
Photograph courtesy Robert Schoelkopf Gallery,
New York

Louis Féraud's simple classical dress with a lyre motif of 1989 come in the first instance from the Hollywood film fantasy of *Spartacus* and in the second from the real need to transcend the narrow margins of the mundane. The Greek key motif, which Ferguson appropriates from architecture, is a twentieth-century fiction when applied to clothing, a distillation of history that the philosopher Jean Baudrillard sees as the proof of the real. The art of Peter Saari perceives both the ancient object and its preserved state, recognizing the progress of time as a modifying force. Preservation is acknowledged—even in a recreation such as Saari's 1984 untitled work—as a process in which the original appearance changes. Fashion designer Giorgio di Sant'Angelo has made marked use of up-to-date man-made fibers with stretch, yet his evocative work can resemble the gauze clothing and wrapped mummies of ancient Egypt or the semblance of wet drapery in the clothing and sculpture of ancient Greece. For di Sant'Angelo, a contemporary collection is endowed with echoes of the past for those who perceive them but allows an uncompromised sense of the present for those who do not.

Though most of the examples considered so far draw their inspiration across a great chronological distance, it has also been clear during the 1980s that the more recent past provides important historical touchstones. Henry James understood the compelling presence of such a past when in 1888 he wrote in the Preface to *The Aspern Papers:*

> I delight in a palpable imaginable *visitable* past—in the nearer distance and the clearer mysteries, the marks and signs of a world we may reach over to as by making a long arm we grasp an object at the other end of our own table. That, to my imagination, is a past fragrant of all, or of almost all, the poetry of the thing outlived and lost and gone, and yet in which the precious element of closeness, telling so of connections but tasting so of differences, remains appreciable.

In 1985, drawing on a past not strictly visitable for many of us, designer Norma Kamali extended an invitation to voyage some seven decades back in time, a time demonstrably removed from our own styles, mores, and manner of dress, though not entirely removed from our mind's eye. Kamali's solicitation is historicist in a traditional way. Perhaps this historicism seems anomalous for a designer as directional and, as one would have said some years ago, as revolutionary as Kamali. In fact, her oeuvre provides a fine illustration of the recent journey from Modernism to historicism. In the 1970s, Kamali responded to the dictates of function, fashion, radicalism, and the inherent properties of materials. These Modernist attributes were less evident in her work of the 1980s. The historically resonant designs she offered in that decade represent a fundamental change in her approach, a change that does not, as some cynics might suggest, reflect a clientele less young or a sensibility less sharp, but is rather a reflection of the past, appropriate in the context of contemporary design.

The power of Henry James's observations on the visitable past becomes even clearer as the historical object on "our own table" becomes closer. The past just before our time, of which we are capable of recollection, and the present that is a reinterpretation and representation of that past make a fascinating juxtaposition. Marc Jacobs, Stephen Sprouse, and Thierry Mugler—three designers who celebrate themes of the 1960s and 1970s—have been attracted by this challenge. Their evocations of the immediate past illustrate how important the delicate tissue of generations became for artists and designers in the 1980s. They rightly perceive that today artists and designers visit their own remembered and barely remembered pasts with a special

Norma Kamali. Faille Coatdress, Spring–Summer Collection, 1985–86. Courtesy the designer

Marc Jacobs. Happy Face Sweater, Fall–Winter Collection, 1985–86. Courtesy Fairchild Syndication. Photograph George Chinsee

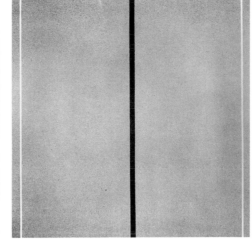

Barnett Newman. *Who's Afraid of Red, Yellow, and Blue II*, 1967. Acrylic on canvas. Private collection

Philip Taaffe. *We Are Not Afraid* (after Barnett Newman), 1985. Linoprint, collage, and acrylic on canvas. Courtesy Pat Hearn Gallery, New York

David Diao. *Painting in 21 Parts* (after installation view of paintings by Kasimir Malevich in the "Last Futurist Exhibition 0.10," Petrograd, 1915). Acrylic on canvas. Courtesy Postmasters, New York

David McDermott and Peter McGough. *1917*, 1988. Oil on linen and wood. Courtesy Massimo Audiello Gallery, New York

clarity and powerful sentiment.

Some artists of the 1980s betray a like fascination with the 1950s and '60s. Artist Philip Taaffe's *We Are Not Afraid*, of 1985, for example, is a response, delayed by almost twenty years, to Barnett Newman's painting of 1967 entitled *Who's Afraid of Red, Yellow, and Blue II*. Taaffe's work is engaged in a dialogue with a painting done when he was in elementary school. It is as if today's art bore an intimate engagement with the past. When Taaffe twists Newman's disengaged and uninflected stripes, his artistic stance is open and ironic. At the same time he reminds us that memory is a cognitive and—of course—an interpretive process. Taaffe's statement is echoed in fashion design by Moschino's caricatures of Hippie clothing and by Dorothée Bis and Carolyne Roehm's witty versions of 1960s minidresses. They all serve to reformulate the more recent past in the same manner as do historicizing works of art.

Coming on the heels of Modernist supremacy, the historicist forays in the art and design communities raise an inevitable question of some urgency. Does the present become a passive agent when we recognize, even venerate, the past with the eyes of our own time? The answer must be no. To simulate the past does not capture it. In fact, the very simulation demonstrates that the past is ever elusive. To wear or approximate the clothing of another era is not time travel in the manner of Jules Verne. Dressed and resident in the styles of the past, artist-collaborators David McDermott and Peter McGough create art in a like archaism that may strive for history but never quite leaves the present. The same can be said of the historicist architecture and furniture of the 1980s. Anthony Burgess, the novelist who in 1962 offered a horrific specter of the future in *A Clockwork Orange*, some twenty years later became engrossed in history and the historical novel. In a 1985 justification of the preoccupation Burgess said: "The past is made by the present. The pattern we call history is not history, it's made by us." This pattern of history can form new buildings, inspire new Hepplewhite and Chippendale chairs, cut new garments, and perhaps even craft a new world.

The excitement of 1980s historicism also raises the question of imitation. Copies of early-twentieth-century paintings by Ilya Chasnik, Kasimir Malevich, and Pablo Picasso, or even more recent work by Roy Lichtenstein, by such artists as Sherrie Levine, David Diao, Mike Bidlo, and Elaine Sturtevant have posed the problems of sound and echo in contemporary art. But the inspirational borrowing across art's distant and recent generations is not plagiarism. An object or concept is transformed by its time travel. A work of contemporary art or design answers the charge of plagiarism with alterations in material or context. It asserts différence despite likeness. In clothing the garment is not replicated in the manner of copying but in assimilation. Elements are borrowed, but differentiation is supreme. When painter Russell Connor recreates masterpieces in interpretive juxtapositions—confronting Manet with Manet in *The Opening*, 1988, and Rubens with Picasso in *The Kidnapping of Modern Art by the New Yorkers*, 1985—or when Mark Tansey offers art a revisionist history through its own images, especially of the Modernist masters, the cognitive displacement of the original image with the new, as in *Source of the Loue* (after Courbet), 1988, is effective. Christian Lacroix adapts a late 1860s walking dress, exaggerating it to make it look like a later form. In a seventeenth-century-style dress, French couturier Maryll Lanvin performs a like act of disorienting two discrete forms through the placement of a laced bodice with a related but ordinarily irreconcilable image: a separate high neck. Lanvin's seventeenth-century dress is as plausible as Connor's interpretive art history, yet on

Edouard Manet. *The Bar at the Folies-Bergère,* 1881–82. Oil on canvas. Courtauld Institute Galleries, London

Russell Connor. *The Opening* (after Edouard Manet), 1988. Oil on canvas. Courtesy the artist

Edouard Manet. *Le Déjeuner sur l'herbe*, 1862–63. Oil on canvas. Musée du Louvre, Paris

Maryll Lanvin for Lanvin. Evening Gown, Fall–Winter Collection, 1988–89. Photograph courtesy *Collezioni*, Zanfi Editore, S.r.l.

Cover, *Artforum*, April 1986. Rococo period room
at The Metropolitan Museum of Art, New York,
with section of tapestry at right replaced by detail
of General Idea's *Le Fin*, 1985

Mark Tansey. *Source of the Loue* (after Gustave
Courbet), 1988. Oil on canvas. Courtesy Curt
Marcus Gallery, New York

examination the parts of the dress are not integrated and would
never have come together but for the artist-designer's imposed
anachronism. It is a fine illustration of how historicism's petty thefts
lead to a bright and original creative conclusion.

The April 1986 cover of the magazine *Artforum* replaces an
image within a Rococo period room at The Metropolitan Museum
of Art in New York with another by General Idea from 1985. The
anachronistic image may justly be said to alter our perception of all
the surrounding images and of the Rococo room itself. But has
anything really changed? When Romeo Gigli instills the cocoon
shape of a 1920s coat and the soft chiffon of an Empire dress with
an attitude distinctly 1980s, the result can only diminish our historical distance from the sources Gigli taps with the knowledge and
adaptability of a virtuoso. Similarly, Christian Lacroix's prodigious
historicism in his evocations of jewel-encrusted Byzantine splendor
and of eighteenth-century extravagance suggests both the historian's delight in knowledge and the artist's command of diverse
styles.

Dwight Culler's 1985 book *The Victorian Mirror of History* reflects
upon Victorian England's vision of the past. Culler recognizes that
the past served both individual and collective self-knowledge in the
Victorian age, its historical comprehensions defining the characteristics of the time and the meaning of individual lives in the period.
Culler summarizes the Victorian epoch:

> It read history for its bearing upon the present, but in the course
> of reading it educated itself and so was better prepared to offer
> new, creative solutions of its own. Indeed, in the course of
> looking to the past it became conscious of the distinctive charac-
> teristics of the present. It was by the process of searching
> through the past for analogies to its own situation and becoming
> aware that there was a certain sense in which Thucydides,
> Lucretius, and Botticelli were "modern," whereas Herodotus,
> Cicero, and Raphael were not, that the Victorians became
> conscious of the true meaning of modernity and of the charac-
> teristics of their own age.

Indeed what Culler says of the Victorian age may also be true of
the historicism in our time; it is a process of evaluation, analogy, and
differentiation that allows us to understand modernity and to
realize the characteristics of our own age. In this process, our
retrospection is a kind of introspection; our fascination with history
is a means of understanding ourselves.

Fashion is possessed and haunted by its acute sense of time. As it
evolves from season to season, it offers a compelling chronometer
of the twentieth century. The 1980s—visually outlined in the pages
that follow—have revealed a new measure with which to perceive
a past in tandem with the present, not just in fashion but also in
painting and sculpture. An unremitting modernism—a long
standing cult of the new—has seemingly come to a rapprochement
with memory and an alliance with history.

Antiquity and

Early Christian Era

2000 B.C.—A.D. 1400

Francis Parkman, in describing the nature of history and the obliga-
tions of the historian, argued: "Faithfulness to the truth of history
involves far more than a research, however patient and scrupulous,
into special facts. Such facts may be detailed with the most minute
exactness, and yet the narrative, taken as a whole, may be un-
meaning or untrue. The narrator must seek to imbue himself with
the life and spirit of the time. He must study events in their bearings
near and remote; in the character, habits, and manners of those
who took part in them. He must himself be, as it were, a sharer or
a spectator of the action he describes" (*Pioneers of France in the
New World*, 1865). Even at its greatest chronological remove,
history beckons the contemporary artist and designer offering
the principles that once animated the Egyptian Revival, Gustave
Courbet's Assyrianism, and the unending series of neoclassicisms
and neomedievalisms.

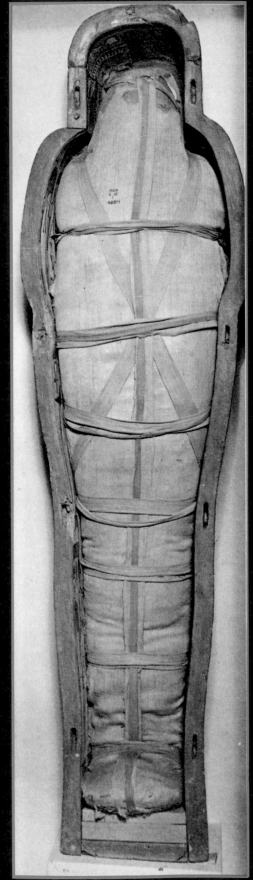

Mummy of a Priestess. New York Public
Library, Picture Collection

Ann McCoy, *Barque with Lion Goddess III*, 1985.
Bronze. Courtesy Brooke Alexander, Inc., New
York

Mark Innerst. Untitled (Memnon), 1984. Oil on
board. Courtesy Curt Marcus Gallery, New York

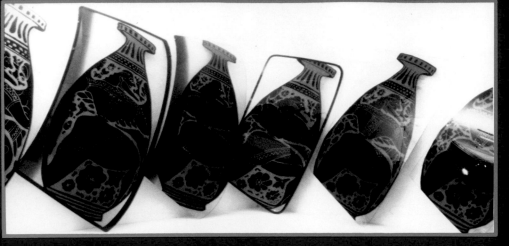

ANCIENT GREECE

Louis Féraud. Lyre Gown, Spring–Summer Collection, 1989. Photograph courtesy *Collezioni* Zanfi Editore, S.r.1.

Maura Sheehan. *The Bearded Lady* (detail), 1985. Paint on shattered automobile windshields. Courtesy Barbara Flynn Gallery, New York. Photograph Alan Porter

Athenian Oil Flask (detail), third quarter of the Century B.C. Private collection

Stanley Tigerman. Pediment Chair, 1982. Epoxy-finished steel. Courtesy the designer

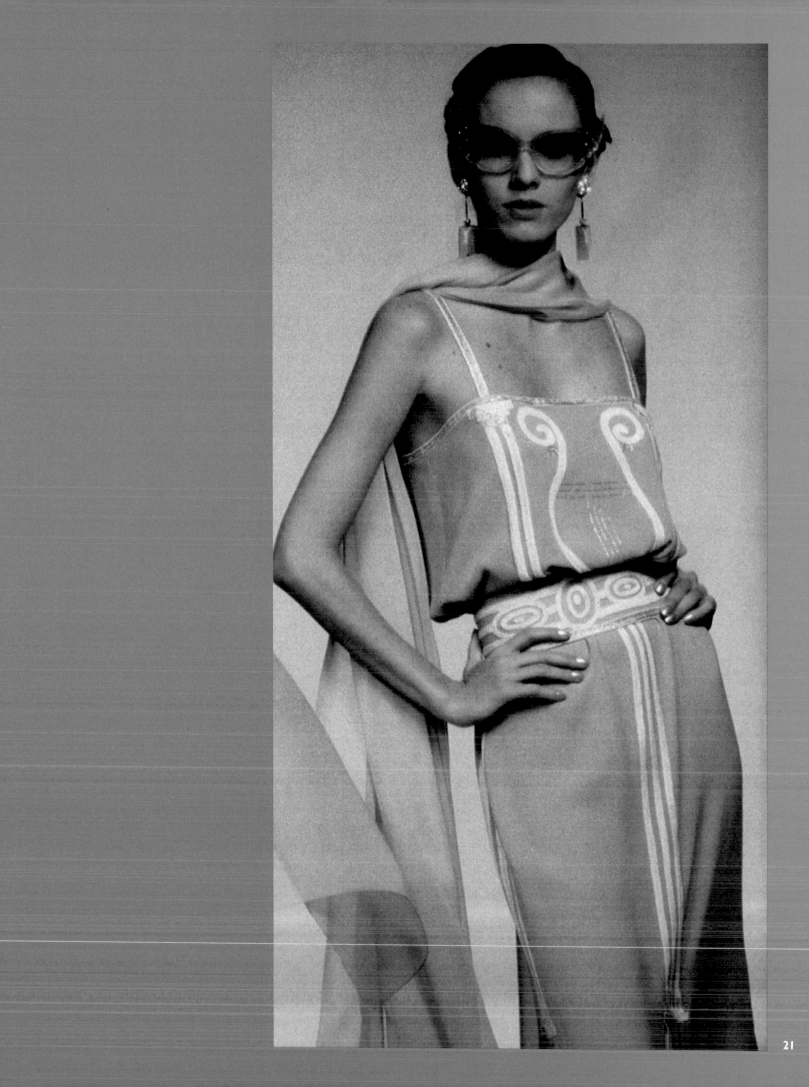

Giorgio di Sant'Angelo. Draped Evening Gowns
Spring–Summer Collection, 1989. Photograph
Cindy Sirko

Anne and Patrick Poirier. *Pegasus,* 1984. Mixed
media. Courtesy Sonnabend Gallery, New York

Tanagra Statuette, 3rd Century B.C. Terracotta.
Musée du Louvre, Paris

ANCIENT GREECE

Angel Estrada. Draped Evening Gown, Spring–
Summer Collection, 1989. Photograph courtesy
Collezioni, Zanfi Editore, S.r.l.

Edward Allington. *Tamed Time/Aphrodite ad
Infinitum*, 1986. Plaster casts and stuccoed wood.
Courtesy Diane Brown Gallery, New York

Artemis (detail from Parthenon frieze), 5th
Century B.C. Acropolis Museum, Athens

Bill Sullivan for Chelsea Custom Corporation.
Bench, 1988. Poplar with hand-painted finish

Maura Sheehan. *Elapsed Time* (detail of installation),
1986–87. Clay and volcanic dust from Pompeii.
Courtesy Barbara Flynn Gallery, New York

ANCIENT GREECE

Douglas Ferguson. Mesh Evening Dresses, 1985.
Photograph Josef Astor

Roger Brown. *Galvanized Temple*, 1985. Aluminum
Courtesy Phyllis Kind Gallery, New York

Athenian Krater (detail of Actaeon) from Cumae,
5th Century B.C. Museum of Fine Arts, Boston

Peter Saari. Untitled, 1985. Casein and gouache
with plaster on canvas, mounted on wood.
Courtesy Robert Schoelkopf Gallery, New York.
Photograph D. James Dee

BYZANTINE EMPIRE

Mary McFadden. Evening Gown, 1986. Photograph Marcus Leatherdale

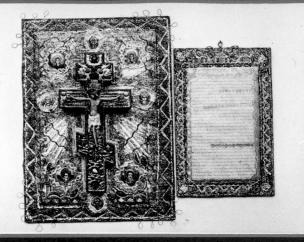

Thomas Lanigan-Schmidt. *A Child's Byzantium in New Jersey*, 1982. Mixed media. Courtesy Holly Solomon Gallery, New York

Consecration of San Vitale (detail of Empress Theodora), 6th Century. Mosaic. San Vitale, Ravenna

BYZANTINE EMPIRE

Christian Lacroix. Embroidered Jacket, Fall–Winter
Collection, 1988–89. Photograph courtesy
Collezioni, Zanfi Editore S.r.1.

The Emperor John Cantacuzenus, 14th Century.
Manuscript. Bibliothèque Nationale, Paris

Ron Janowich. *Byzantium*, 1985. Black oil on linen.
Courtesy Galerie Lelong, New York

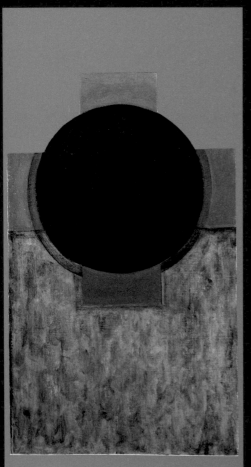

The Great Tradition

1400–1800

As history's great chronicle unfolded, its patterns and its logic became subject to the disputations of ethics, philosophy, and poetry. "Eternall Providence" and like manifestations of destiny seemed to give history not merely an outline but a precise configuration. Although Walter Pater averred in writing of the Renaissance that "every intellectual product must be judged from the point of view of the age and the people in which it was produced" (*The History of the Renaissance*, 1873), his great paradigm was itself a revival of Classical Antiquity, itself a reminder that renewal is the quintessential historical experience.

Franck Joseph Bastille. Bridal Dress, Fall–Winter Collection, 1988–89. Photograph Josef Astor

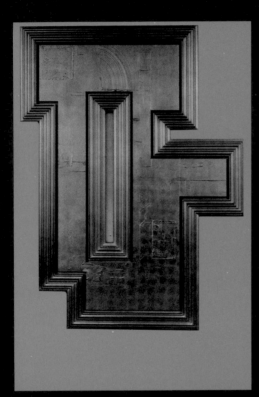

Christian Eckart. *Andachtsbild #703*, 1987. Gold leaf over gel medium on birch plywood and on pine and poplar frame. Courtesy Massimo Audiello Gallery, New York. Photograph Tom Warren

Carlo Braccesco. *Annunciation* (detail of the Virgin), late 15th Century. Musée du Louvre, Paris

Michael Abrams. *Diadem*, 1988. Mixed media on wood. Courtesy Trabia-MacAfee Gallery, New York

Piero and Antonio Pollaiuolo. *Galeazzo Maria Sforza*, c. 1470–76. Oil. Galleria degli Uffizi, Florence

Ron Janowich. *St. Augustine*, 1984. Black oil on linen. Courtesy Galerie Lelong, New York

Reedspear Tournament at Valladolid (detail), 1506. Private collection, Ecaussines

Jean-Paul Gaultier. Heraldic Jacket, Spring–Summer Collection, 1988. Photograph Josef Astor

Saint Clair Cemin. *We Franciscans*, 1986. Bronze, steel, and tatami mat. Courtesy Massimo Audiello Gallery, New York

Illustration of Spanish House Coat, from Christoph Weiditz, *Das Trachtenbuch*, 1529. Germanisches Nationalmuseum, Nuremberg

Robert Colescott. *Knowledge of the Past Is the Key to the Future* (*St. Sebastian*), 1986. Acrylic on canvas. Courtesy Phyllis Kind Gallery, New York

Hans Funk. Design for an Armorial Window, for Jacob Mey (detail), 1532. Pen and ink with wash, heightened with color. Kunsthaus, Zürich

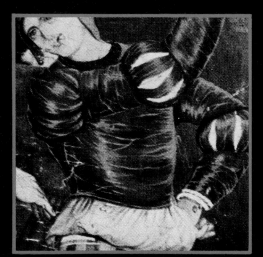

Ororbia Master. *The Flagellation of Christ* (detail of the Flagellator), c. 1530. Fresco. Parish Church, Ororbia, Spain

Les Quatre Fils Aymon: Marriage of Renaud de Montauban and Clarisse (detail), c. 1450. Manuscript. Bibliothèque de l'Arsenal, Paris

René d'Anjou. *Traité de la forme et devis d'un tournoi* (detail of the presentation of the sword), c. 1460–65. Bibliothèque Nationale, Paris

Mark Tansey. *Triumph over Mastery*, 1987. Oil on canvas. Courtesy Curt Marcus Gallery, New York

Andrea Mantegna. *Ludovico III Gonzaga among His Relatives* (detail), 1471–74. Ducal Palace, Mantua, Camera degli Sposi

Russell Connor. *The Kidnapping of Modern Art by the New Yorkers*, 1985. Oil on canvas. Private collection.

Young Unmarried Woman from Saxony, from Hans Weigel, *Das Trachtenbuch: Habitus*, 1577

SIXTEENTH CENTURY

Maryll Lanvin for Lanvin. Evening Gown, Fall–Winter Collection, 1988–89. Photograph David Seidner. Courtesy Lanvin

Tibor Csernus. *Urias*, 1988. Oil on canvas. Courtesy Claude Bernard Gallery, New York

Catherine de Médicis (detail), late 16th Century. Tapestry. Galleria degli Uffizi, Florence

Karl Lagerfeld for Chanel. Evening Dress, Fall–
Winter Collection, 1988–89. Photograph courtesy
Collezioni, Zanfi Editore, S.r.1.

Mary Hill (Mrs. Mackwilliam), c. 1585–90. Oil on
panel. Private collection

Isaac Oliver. *Portrait of an* [...]
late 16th Century. Water[...]
Her Majesty The Queen[...]

ELIZABETHAN AGE

Zandra Rhodes. Evening Gown, Fall–Winter Collection, 1981. Victoria and Albert Museum, London. Photograph Josef Astor

Mary Fitton, c. 1595. Oil on canvas. Private collection

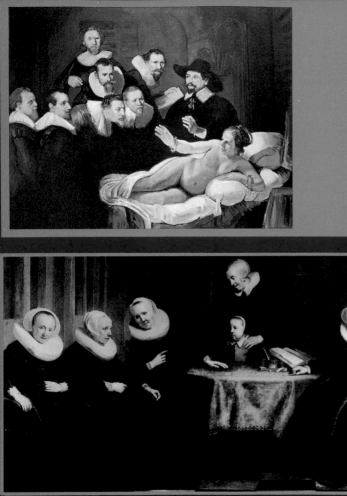

Franco Moschino. Pants Ensemble, Fall–Winter Collection, 1988–89. Photograph courtesy the designer

Russell Connor. "*What Do Women Want?*" 1985. Oil on canvas. Private collection

Jacob Backer. *Regentesses of the Burgher Orphanage, Amsterdam* (detail), 1633–34. Oil on canvas. Historisch Museum, Amsterdam

Maryll Lanvin for Lanvin. Dinner Dress, Fall–Winter Collection, 1988–89. Photograph Josef Astor

Barbara Bloom. *The Reign of Narcissism* (detail of installation), 1988–89. Mixed media. Courtesy Jay Gorney Modern Art, New York, and Isabella Kacprzak, Cologne, West Germany

Anthony van Dyke. *The Abbé Scalia* (detail), 1634–35. Oil on canvas. Private collection

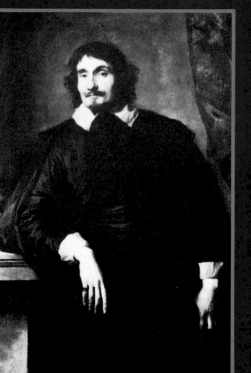

Karl Lagerfeld for Chanel. Evening Knickers Ensemble, Fall–Winter Collection, 1987–88. Photograph courtesy *HiFashion*

Mark Innerst. *Venetian Ceiling*, 1988. Acrylic on board. Courtesy Curt Marcus Gallery, New York

Costume design for Louis XIV as Sun King, in the *Ballet de Nuit*, c. 1653, by Jean-Baptiste Lully

Elizabeth and David Emanuel. Evening Dress, 198
Photograph Marc Vodofsky. Courtesy and
Copyright © *New York Post*

Michael Abrams. *The Expulsion*, 1985. Mixed
media. Courtesy Trabia-MacAfee Gallery,
New York

Jean-Baptiste Santerre. *Marie Adelaide Savoie,
Duchess of Burgundy*, 1709. Oil on canvas. Musée
de Versailles

Karl Lagerfeld for Chanel. Evening Pants Ensemble,
Spring–Summer Collection, 1985. Photograph
Guy Marineau. Courtesy *Women's Wear Daily*,
Fairchild Syndication, New York

Joan Nelson. Untitled (162), 1987. Oil on wood.
Private collection

Antoine Watteau. *Pierrot* (called *Gilles*) (detail),
c. 1718–19. Oil on canvas. Musée du Louvre, Paris

Antoine Watteau. *The Shop Sign*, or *Gersaint's Shop Sign* (detail), c. 1720. Oil on canvas. Schloss Charlottenburg, Berlin

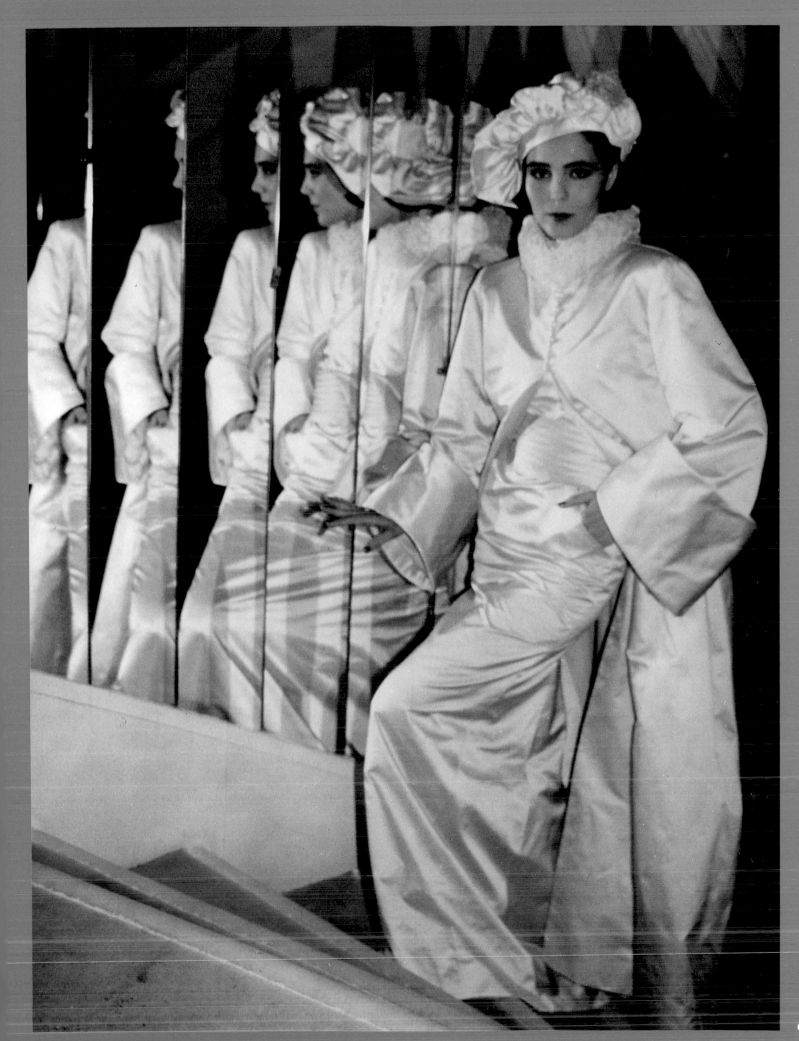

EARLY EIGHTEENTH CENTURY

Karl Lagerfeld for Chanel. Evening Dress, Fall–
Winter Collection, 1987–88. Photograph courtesy
HiFashion

Joan Nelson. Untitled (180), 1988. Oil on wood.
Private collection

Antoine Watteau. *French Comedians* (detail),
c. 1720–21. Oil on canvas. The Metropolitan
Museum of Art, New York, Jules Bache Collection

Elizabeth and David Emanuel. Evening Dress, 1989.
Photograph Marc Vodofsky. Courtesy and
Copyright © *New York Post*

Peter Nagy. *Belief in Style*, 1988. Acrylic on canvas.
Collection John L. Stewart

H. Pauquet. *Dance*, 1763. Engraving

Christian Lacroix. Evening Pants Ensemble, Fall–Winter Collection, 1988–89. Photograph courtesy Lesage, Paris

Frankenthal. *Columbine as Female Harlequin*, c. 1758. Porcelain. Pauls Collection, Basel

Quilted Petticoat, late 18th Century
Sturbridge Village, Sturbridge, Mass.

Quilted Petticoat (detail)

Fashion Plate. *Le Journal des dames*
late 18th Century

Man's Ensemble, c. 1785. Embroidered velvet and silk satin. Musée des Arts de la Mode, Paris, UFAC. Photograph David Seidner

Carle Vernet. *Parisian Incroyable*, c. 1790–1800.
Drawing. Musée du Louvre, Paris, Cabinet des
Dessins

The Modern Heritage

"Mankind," said Robert Louis Stevenson, "was never so happily inspired as when it made a cathedral" (*An Inland Voyage*, 1878). The modern era revisits the dreams of the Golden Age and of purportedly ideal times before the revolutions of peoples, technology, and cities. Largely accepting the jeremiads of civilization's decline, the modern era has oscillated between defiant self-confidence and modern doubt, insisting upon a preferred past.

Romeo Gigli. Evening Dress, Spring–Summer Collection, 1987. Photograph Paolo Roversi. Courtesy the designer

French artist. *Mlle Charlotte du Val d'Ognes*, c. 1810. Oil on canvas. The Metropolitan Museum of Art, New York

Eugène Delacroix. *Liberty Leading the People* (detail of Liberty), 1830. Oil on canvas. Musée du Louvre, Paris

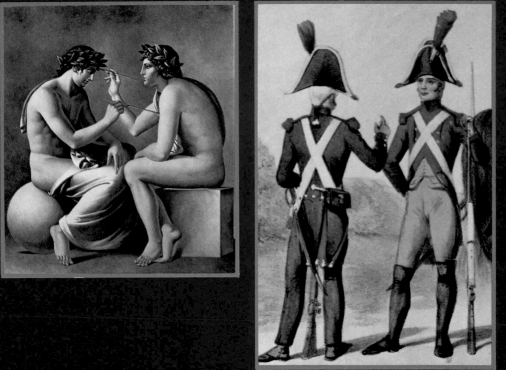

Carlo Maria Mariani. *Il mano ubbidisce all'intelle*
1983. Oil on canvas. Courtesy Sperone
Westwater, New York

Garde impériale (detail), 1806. Print

Dottie Attie. *In Old Age He Painted*, 1986. Pencil on paper. Courtesy P.P.O.W. Gallery, New York

Jean-Auguste-Dominique Ingres. *M. Charles-Marie-Jean-Baptiste-François Marcotte d'Argenteuil*, Rome, 1810. Drawing

Jean-Auguste-Dominique Ingres. *M. Cordier* (detail), 1811. Oil on canvas. Musée du Louvre, Paris

Fashion Plate: Gentlemen's Fashions (detail: Riding Dress), June 1833. Fashion Institute of Technology, New York, Special Collections

Frédéric Bazille. *Family Gathering* (detail). 1869. Oil on canvas. Musée du Louvre, Paris

Mark Innerst. *Reservoir*, 1986. Watercolor on paper. Courtesy Curt Marcus Gallery, New York

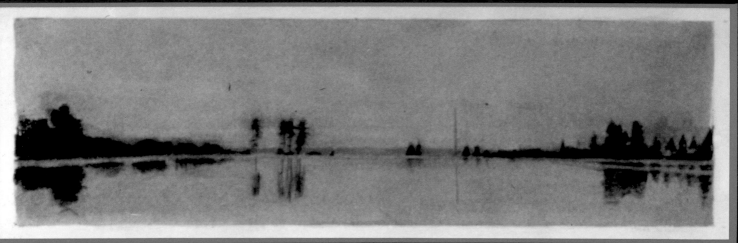

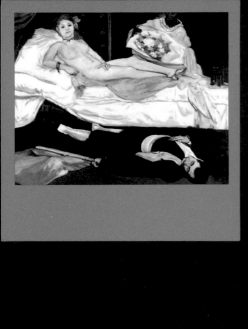

Russell Connor. *Love and Death*, 1984. Oil on canvas. Collection the artist

Home, Walking, and Children's Dresses (detail). *Harper's Bazar*, January 18, 1868

Mark Innerst. *Paintings*, 1988. Acrylic and phototransfer on canvas. Courtesy Curt Ma[...] Gallery, New York

James Tissot. *Too Early*, 1873. Oil on canvas. Guildhall Art Gallery, London

Christian Lacroix. Wedding Gown, Fall–Winter
Collection, 1987–88. Photograph Roxanne Lowit

The Caprice Jacket. *The Queen*, September 23,
1882

Fashion Plate, 1885

Cashmere House Gown. *Harper's Baz*
October 30, 1897

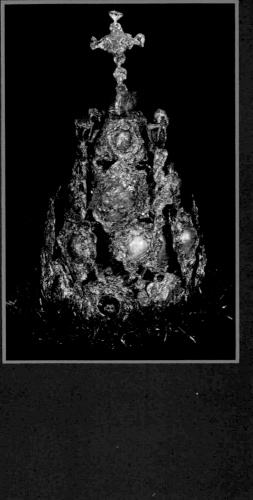

Thomas Lanigan-Schmidt. *Czar's Crown Made from Leftover Aluminum Foil and Plastic Wrap*, 1983. Mixed media. Courtesy Holly Solomon Gallery, New York

Fashion Plate. *La Moda Elegante Ilustrada*, November 30, 1898

A Visitable Past

In describing the American strain of man in the twentieth century, Thomas Wolfe wrote: "The young men of this land are not, as they are often called, a 'lost' race—they are a race that never yet has been discovered. And the whole secret, power, and knowledge of their own discovery is locked within them—they know it, feel it, have the whole thing in them—and they cannot utter it" (*The Web and the Rock*, 1930). The century that has unveiled the mystique of progress has instead discerned a past, both collective and individual, that in being not yet discovered is the ultimate quest.

Charles Dana Gibson. Golfing (detail of a Gibson Girl), c. 1900

Mitsuhiro Matsuda for Matsuda. Suit, Spring–
Summer Collection, 1989. Photograph Josef

Fashion Plate: Beach Ensembles. *Femina*, July
1909

Mike Bidlo. *Not Picasso*, 1983. Oil on canvas.
Courtesy Bruno Bischofberger, Zürich

Fashion Plate. *La Moda Elegante Ilustrada*,
December 22, 1907

Giorgio Armani. Evening Dress, Spring–Summer
Collection, 1989. Photograph courtesy the
designer

Gertrude Vanderbilt Whitney in Bakst Tunic, 1913.
Courtesy Mrs. Thomas Leboutillier. Photograph
Baron de Meyer

Women's Auxiliary Corps, 1918

Fashion Plate. *La Moda Elegante Ilustrada*
November 22, 1917

Mme Poiret wearing "La Faune," 1919. Musée des Arts de la Mode, Paris, UFAC. Photograph Man Ray

Romeo Gigli. Coat, Fall–Winter Collection, 1989–90. Photograph courtesy the designer

Louise Lawler. *In the Home of a Friend of Léger, Paris,*1985. Black-and-white photograph and mat with transfer type. Courtesy Metro Pictures, New York

Leslie L. Saalburg. Fashion Plate. *Vogue,* March 15, 1922

Franco Moschino. Evening Dress, Spring–Summer
Collection, 1989. Photograph courtesy Moschino

Louise Lawler. *MoMA, December 1985*, 1985.
Photograph. Courtesy Metro Pictures, New York

Illustration, Black Voile Dress by Chanel. *Vogue*
(Paris), January 1927

Komar and Melamid. *The Origin of Socialist Realism*, 1982–83. Oil on canvas. Courtesy Ronald Feldman Fine Arts, Inc., New York

Howard and Joan Coster. *Miss Margaret Whigham of Ascot* (later Duchess of Argyll), 1931. Photograph *Vogue*, 1931

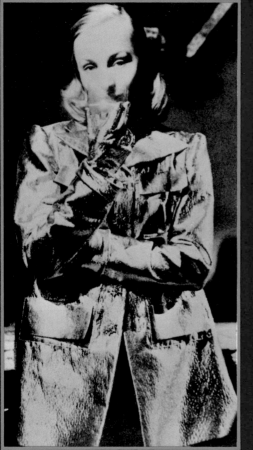

Hoyningen–Huene. Gold-lamé Re
Photograph *Harper's Bazaar*, 1939

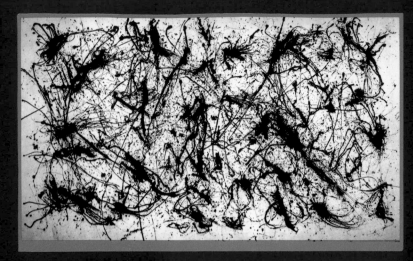

John Galliano. Suit, Spring–Summer Collection, 1989. Photograph Vallhonrat. Courtesy the designer

Mike Bidlo. *Not Pollock (Number 32, 1950)*, 1983. Enamel on canvas. Collection the artist

Charles James, 1949. Photograph Cecil Beaton. Courtesy Sotheby's, London

Chanel. Suit with Gilt Buttons, 1963. Photograph
Hatami

Paco Rabanne. Minidress, c. 1968. Fashion Institute
of Technology, New York, Edward C. Blum Design
Laboratory. Photograph Irving Solero

Elaine Sturtevant. *Lichtenstein Study for Frightened Girl*, 1988. Graphite and colored pencil on paper. Courtesy Bess Cutler Gallery, New York

Pierre Cardin. Dress, 1966–67. Fashion Institute of Technology, New York, Edward C. Blum Design Laboratory. Photograph Irving Solero

Sly Stone in Halston Jumpsuit, June 197[.]
Photograph Oscar Abolafía

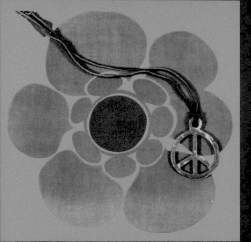

Peace Medallion, c. 1970. Fashion Institute of
Technology, New York, Edward C. Blum Design
Laboratory. Photograph Irving Solero

153

Boy. T-Shirt, Vest, Miniskirt, and Cap Ensemble, Spring–Summer Collection, 1989. Photograph courtesy *Collezioni*, Zanfi Editore, S.r.1.

Kenny Scharf. *Felix on a Pedestal*, 1982. Acrylic and spray paint on canvas. Collection Mr. and Mrs. Ara Arslanian. Courtesy Tony Shafrazi Gallery, New York

Tie-dyed T-shirt and Leather Vest, 1969–72. Fashion Institute of Technology, New York, Edward C. Blum Design Laboratory. Photograph Irving Solero

Guy Paulin. Day Dress, Spring-Summer Collection,
1988 (see page 79). Photograph Josef Astor

Baines, Barbara Burman. *Fashion Revivals: From the Elizabethan Age to the Present Day.* London, 1981.

Bard College, Annandale-on-Hudson, New York. *Neo Neo-Classicism: The Uses of Tradition in Late 20th Century Art,* essay by Deborah Drier. Annandale-on-Hudson, New York, 1986.

Barthes, Roland. *The Rustle of Language,* translated by Richard Howard. New York, 1986.

Baudrillard, Jean. *Simulations.* New York, 1983.

Belting, Hans. *The End of the History of Art?* Chicago, 1987.

Braudel, Fernand. *On History.* Chicago, 1980.

Cohn, Norman. *The Pursuit of the Millennium.* New York, rev. ed. 1970.

Culler, Dwight. *The Victorian Mirror of History.* New York, 1985.

Eco, Umberto. *Art and Beauty in the Middle Ages.* New Haven, Connecticut, 1986. First published Milan, 1959.

_____. *Postscript to the Name of the Rose.* New York, 1984.

_____. *Travels in Hyperreality.* New York, 1986.

Halley, Peter. *Collected Essays, 1981–87.* Zürich, 1988.

Honour, Hugh. *Neo-Classicism.* New York, 1968; rev. ed. 1977.

Institute of Contemporary Art, Boston. *Endgame: Reference and Simulation in Recent Painting and Sculpture.* Boston, 1986.

Jencks, Charles. *The Language of Post Modern Architecture.* New York and London, 1977.

_____. *Post-Modernism: The New Classicism in Art and Architecture.* New York and London, 1987.

Krieger, Murray, ed. *The Aims of Representation.* New York, 1987.

Lyotard, Jean-François. *The Postmodern Condition: A Report on Knowledge.* Manchester, 1984.

The Museum of Contemporary Art, Los Angeles. *A Forest of Signs: Art in the Crisis of Representation,* edited by Catherine Gudis; essays by Ann Goldstein, Mary Jane Jacob, and Anne Rorimer. Los Angeles and Cambridge, Massachusetts, 1989.

New Museum of Contemporary Art, New York. *The Art of Memory: The Loss of History,* essays by David Deitcher, William Olander, and Abigail Solomon-Godeau. New York, 1985.

Popper, Karl R. *The Poverty of Historicism.* London, 1957.

Portoghesi, Paolo. *Postmodern: The Architecture of the Postindustrial Society.* New York, 1983.

Representations (University of California Press, Berkeley) 26. Special Issue: Memory and Counter-Memory. Spring 1989.

San Francisco Museum of Art. *Second Sight: Biennial IV,* essay by Graham W. Beale. San Francisco, 1986.

Stern, Robert A. M. *Modern Classicism.* New York, 1989.

Toliver, Harold. *The Past That Poets Make.* Cambridge, Massachusetts, 1981.

Veeser, H. Aram, ed. *The New Historicism.* New York, 1988.

Venturi, Robert. *Complexity and Contradiction in Architecture.* New York, 1966; rev. ed. 1977.

Wallis, Brian, ed. *Art after Modernism: Rethinking Representation.* New York and Boston, 1984.

_____. *Blasted Allegories: An Anthology of Writings by Contemporary Artists.* New York, 1987.

White, Hayden. *Tropics of Discourse: Essays in Cultural Criticism.* Baltimore, 1978.

Wilson, Elizabeth. *Adorned in Dreams: Fashion and Modernity.* Berkeley and Los Angeles, 1987.

ACKNOWLEDGMENTS

HRH Queen Elizabeth II
Oscar Abolafia
Michael Abrams
Brooke Alexander, Inc.
Giorgio Armani
    Gabriella Forte
    Tilly Bozzolo
Artforum
Massimo Audiello Gallery
Franck Joseph Bastille
Claude Bernard Gallery
Mike Bidlo
Bruno Bischofberger
Mary Boone Gallery
Boy
Diane Brown Gallery
Byblos
    Alan Cleaver
    Keith Varty
    Sabrina Pigola
Isabel Canovas
    Tamsy Smith
Cerruti 1881
    Margaret Muldoon
    Véronique Renault
    Françoise Pommaret
Chanel
    Marie-Louise de Clermont-Tonnerre
    Sophie Lorthiois
    Tracy Lawrence
Chelsea Custom Corporation
    Paul Blitzblau
Alex Chatelain
Collezioni, Zanfi Editore, S.r.l.
    Maria Grazia Bassissi
    Celestino Zanfi
Condé-Nast Publications
    Diana Edkins
Russell Connor
Creative Artists Agency
    Fred Spector
Sean Cunningham
Bess Cutler Gallery
Patrick Demarchelier
Christian Dior
    Alexandra Tchernoff-El Khoury
Dorothée Bis
    Jacqueline Jacobson
The Dress
    Amy Downs
Anne Dudley-Ward
Perry Ellis
    Anita Antonini
    Laura Obrian
Emanuel
    David Emanuel
    Elizabeth Emanuel
Angel Estrada
    Anneliese Estrada
Fairchild Publications
    Steve Miller
Fashion Institute of Technology
    Susan Becker

Jane Burns
Barbara Castle
John Corins
Maris Heller
Richard McComb
Janet Ozzard
Dorothy Rudzki
Ellen Shanley
Doris Shapiro
Irving Solero
Tomoko Wheaton
Ronald Feldman Fine Arts
Louis Féraud
    Ghislane Brege
Douglas Ferguson
Gianfranco Ferré
    Luca Colla
    Rita Airaghi
Barbara Flynn Gallery
John Galliano
    Deborah Bulloid
Jean-Paul Gaultier
    Frédérique Lorca
    Frank Chevalier
Romeo Gigli
    Alessandra Alessi
    Giovanna Sala
Jay Gorney Modern Art
    Caroline Roland-Levy
Katharine Hamnett
    Nick Vinson
Harpers & Queen
    Susanna van Langenberg
Hermès
    Falvie Chaillet
    Michele Gozland
HiFashion
    Yoko Hamada
Charles Jencks
Betsey Johnson
    Lisa Decker
Johnson Burgee Architects
    Joy Brandon
Marie-Andrée Jouve
Kashiyama
    Irma Botier
Keeble Cavaco & Duka
    Allie Daley
Phyllis Kind Gallery
Knoll International
    Carol Kim
Christian Lacroix
    Jean-Jacques Picart
Lanvin
    Maryll Lanvin
    Véronique Benard-Vilnet
    Eric Turmel
Marcus Leatherdale
Mrs. Thomas Leboutillier
Galerie Lelong
Albert Lesage et Cie
    François Lesage
Daniel Levine

Nathaniel Lieberman
Roxanne Lowit
Curt Marcus Gallery
    Gordon Veneklasen
Matsuda
    Linda Sarro
Mary McFadden
    Larry Deemer
Metro Pictures
Metropolitan Museum of Art
Nando Miglia, S.r.l.
    Ramona Rossi
Issey Miyake
    Jun Kanai
Moda and Company
    Ed Riley
William Morris Agency
    John Planco
Moschino
    Massimo Storni
    Lida Castelli
Thierry Mugler
    Alix Malka
Musée des Arts de la Mode, UFAC
    Florence Müller
Musée de l'Impression sur Etoffes
New York Post
    Carol Lee
L'Officiel Hommes
    Marie Josi
Old Sturbridge Village
    Mary Baker-Wood
OMO Norma Kamali
    Janet Youngren
P.P.O.W. Gallery
Park Tower Development
    Candace Burtis
Guy Paulin
    Stephanie Bernardo
    Mlle Melloule
Postmasters Gallery
Anthony Price
Zandra Rhodes
    Gill Curry
Rizzoli International Publications
    William Dworkin
    Mara Lurie
    Peter Mallary
    John Brancati
    Alda Trabucchi
Carolyne Roehm
Yves Saint Laurent
    Stephen de Pietri
Giorgio di Sant'Angelo
    Martin Price
Robert Schoelkopf Gallery
David Seidner
Tony Shafrazi Gallery
Cindy Sirko
Martine Sitbon
    Michele Montagne
Skrebneski
    Jovanna Papadakis

Holly Solomon Gallery
Sonnabend Gallery
Sotheby's, London
    Lydia Cullen
Staten Island Historical Society
    Carol Quinby
Sybilla
    Pedro Paz
    Irene Castaldi
Chantal Thomass
    Mary Anne Cap de Ville
Tigerman McCurry Architects
    Stanley Tigerman
    Sarah Underhill
Town and Country
    Melissa Tardiff
Victoria and Albert Museum
    Avril Hart
    Anne Buddle
British Vogue
    Elaine Shaw
Warner Bros. Inc.
    Judith Singer
Warner/Elecktra/Atlantic Corporation
    Marion Campbell
Nana Watanabe
Albert Watson
    Elizabeth Watson
    Troy Ward
Whitney Museum of American Art
    Noreen Story
Yohji Yamamoto
    Chiaki Yamamura
    Madeline Fukuhara
Sergio Zambon

This book, only a moment in time, attempts to describe history and memory. As such, it benefits from friendships that have endured across three books and that at each point have been purposeful and happy. We are grateful to Charles Davey for his divination of what we had thought we wanted to see and his insight in making it better than we had envisioned it; we are indebted to Jane Fluegel for the care that gives us words and for concepts that give the venture meaning.

In this instance, we enjoyed the great privilege of working with Josef Astor. Accompanied by Lazlo's apt leitmotif "old times . . . not forgotten," his studio transfiguration of garments into dramatic, resonant photographs is a history-defining (and defying) magic. Josef, Chris Smith, and Lazlo have contributed beautiful, lingering images.

Laura Sinderbrand is our wise friend; her intelligence, imagination, and zeal haunt this book, as they reside in our lives.
                                    R.M. and H.K.

Abolafia, Oscar, *150*
Abrams, Michael
  Alchemy, 1989, *11*
  Diadem, 1988, *34*
  The Expulsion, 1985, *64*
Alice Austin at Age Twenty-two,
  1888, *110*
Allington, Edward
  *Tamed Time/Aphrodite ad
    Infinitum*, 1986, *24*
Armani, Giorgio
  Evening dress, 1989, *125*
Artemis, 5th century B.C., *24*
Astor, Josef, *27, 35, 37, 39, 41, 43, 57, 59,
  77, 95, 101, 105, 129, 145*
Artforum, April 1986, cover, *15*
Attie, Dottie
  In Old Age He Painted, 1986, *96*

Backer, Jacob
  *Regentesses of the Burgher
    Orphanage, Amsterdam*, 1633–34, *58*
Ballet de Nuit, c. 1653, by Jean-Baptiste
  Lully, costume design for, *62*
Bastille, Franck Joseph
  Bridal dress, 1988–89, *35*
  Evening pajamas, 1989, *137*
Bazille, Frédéric
  Family Gathering, 1869, *100*
Beaton, Cecil, *142*
Bidlo, Mike
  Not Picasso, 1983, *120*
  Not Pollock (Number 32, 1950),
    1983, *142*
Bis, Dorothée, see Jacobson,
  Jacqueline
Bloom, Barbara
  The Reign of Narcissism, 1988–89, *60*
  The Seven Deadly Sins: Envy, 1988, *8*
Bohan, Marc
  Evening gown, 1987–88, *43*
Boy
  T-shirt, vest, miniskirt, and cap,
    1989, *155*
Braccesco, Carlo
  Annunciation, 15th century, *34*
Brown, Roger
  Galvanized Temple, 1985, *26*
Burne-Jones, Edward
  *The Arming and Departure of the
    Knights of the Round Table on the
    Quest of the Holy Grail*, c. 1890, *10*
Byblos, see Cleaver, Alan, and Varty, Keith

Caprice jacket, 1892, *106*
Cardin, Pierre
  Dress, 1966–67, *148*
Cernin, Saint Clair
  We Franciscans, 1986, *38*
Cerruti, Nino
  Cape and shirt, 1988–89, *95*
Cerruti 1881, see Cerruti, Nino

Chanel, Gabrielle (Coco)
  Black-voile dress, 1927, *134*
  Suit with gilt buttons, 1963, *144*
Chanel, House of, see Lagerfeld, Karl
Chatelain, Alex, *85, 111*
Chelsea Custom Corporation, *74*
Cleaver, Alan, and Keith Varty
  Winter suit, 1988–89, *115*
Colescott, Robert
  *Knowledge of the Past Is the Key to the
    Future*, 1986, *40*
Complice
  Evening dress, 1988–89, *77*
Connor, Russell
  *The Kidnapping of Modern Art by the
    New Yorkers*, 1985, *48*
  Love and Death, 1984, *102*
  The Opening, 1988, *14*
  What Do Women Want?, 1985, *58*
Coster, Howard and Joan, *138*
Csernus, Tibor
  Urias, 1988, *50*

Diao, David
  Painting in 21 Parts, 1985, *13*
Dangerous Liaisons, 1988, film still, *9*
d'Anjou, René
  *Traité de la forme et devis d'un
    tournois*, c. 1460–65, *44*
de Dinan, Aubert
  Fashion plate, 1912, *126*
Delacroix, Eugène
  Liberty Leading the People, 1830, *90*
Demarchelier, Patrick, *97*
de Meyer, Baron Adolphe, *124*
Dior, Christian, House of,
  see Bohan, Marc
di Sant'Angelo, Giorgio
  Draped evening gowns, 1989, *23*
  Wrap dress, 1989, *19*
Dudley-Ward, Anne
  Suit, 1988, *105*

Eckart, Christian
  Andachtsbild #703, 1987, *34*
Emanuel, House of, see Emanuel,
  Elizabeth and David
Emanuel, Elizabeth and David
  Evening dress, 1989, *65*
  Evening dress, 1989, *73*
Estrada, Angel
  Draped evening gown, 1989, *25*

Fashion figures, 1915, *126*
Fashion plates
  Beach ensembles, 1909, *120*
  Dresses, home, walking, and
    children's, 1868, *102*
  Fashion plate, 1885, *106*
  Gentlemen's fashions, 1833, *96*
  Harper's Bazar, 1887, *108*
  Journal des Tailleurs, 1849, *98*

La Moda Elegante Ilustrada, 1898, *114*;
  1907, *120*; 1917, *128*
Le Journal des dames et des modes,
  18th century, *80*
  Spring suit, 1912, *122*
Femina, *120*
Féraud, Louis
  Lyre gown, 1989, *21*
Ferguson, Douglas
  Mesh evening dresses, 1985, *27*
Frankenthal
  Columbine as Female Harlequin,
    c. 1758, *74*
Fujitsuka, Mitsuma, *45, 87*
Funk, Hans
  Armorial window, design for, 1532, *40*

Galliano, John
  Evening gown, 1986, *4*
  Evening gown, 1986, *85*
  Evening gown, 1989, *139*
  Evening gown and coat, 1989, *141*
  Suit, 1989, *143*
Garde impériale, 1806, *92*
Gaultier, Jean-Paul
  Coat, 1988–89, *129*
  Heraldic jacket, 1988, *39*
  Leopard evening bodice, 1988, *41*
  Men's heraldic jackets, 1988, *37*
*Gertrude Vanderbilt Whitney in Bakst
  Tunic*, 1913, *124*
Gibson, Charles Dana
  Golfing, c. 1900, *118*
Gigli, Romeo
  Coat, 1989, *133*
  Evening dress, 1987, *91*
Gillray, James
  A Peep at Christie's, 1796, *84*
Graves, Michael
  Model for Matsuya department store,
    Tokyo, 1982, *10*

Halston
  Jumpsuit, 1974, *150*
Hamnett, Katharine
  Pants ensemble, 1988–89, *99*
Hansen, Beate, *103*
Harper's Bazar, *102, 108, 112*
Hermès
  Riding habit [evening dress], 1986, *97*
  Shirtwaist and skirt, 1989–90, *119*
  House gown, 1897, *112*
Hoyningen-Huene, *140*

Ingres, Jean-Auguste-Dominique
  *M. Charles-Marie-Jean-Baptiste-François
    Marcotte d'Argenteuil*, 1810, *94*
  M. Cordier, 1811, *94*
Innerst, Mark
  Paintings, 1988, *104*
  Reservoir, 1986, *100*
  Untitled (Memnon), 1984, *18*
  Venetian Ceiling, 1988, *62*

Jacobs, Marc
  Happy Face sweater, 1985–86, *12*
Jacobson, Jacqueline
  Minidress, 1988, *147*
James, Charles
  Dress, 1949, *142*
Janowich, Ron
  Byzantium, 1985, *30*
  St. Augustine, 1984, *36*
Jencks, Charles
  Colosseum chair and stool, 1985, *8*
Johnson, Philip, and John Burgee
  33 Maiden Lane, New York, 1986, *10*
Journal des Tailleurs, *98*

Kamali, Norma
  Coat and jacket, 1985, *127*
  Faille coatdress, 1985–86, *12*
Knight, Nick, *109*
Komar and Melamid
  The Origin of Socialist Realism,
    1982–83, *138*
Krater, Athenian, *26*

Lacroix, Christian
  Embroidered jacket, 1988–89, *31*
  Evening pants, 1988–89, *75*
  Wedding gown, 1987–88, *107*
Ladies Home Journal, *122*
Lagerfeld, Karl
  Evening dress, 1985, *81*
  Evening dress, 1987–88, *71*
  Evening dress, 1988–89, *53*
  Evening dress, 1989, *131*
  Evening gown, 1986–87, *103*
  Evening gown, 1988–89, *113*
  Evening gown with Watteau-back coat,
    1985, *9, 69*
  Evening knickers ensemble,
    1987–88, *63*
  Evening pants ensemble, 1985, *67*
  Knickers ensemble, 1988–89, *55*
  Suit, 1989, *123*
La Moda Elegante Ilustrada, *114, 120, 128*
Lanigan-Schmidt, Thomas
  A Child's Byzantium in New Jersey,
    1982, *28*
  *Czar's Crown Made from Leftover
    Aluminum Foil and Plastic Wrap*,
    1983, *114*
Lanvin, House of, see Lanvin, Maryll
Lanvin, Maryll
  Dinner dress, 1988–89, *61*
  Evening dress, 1988–89, *47*
  Evening gown, 1988–89, *14, 49*
  Evening gown, 1988–89, *51*
Lawler, Louise
  In the Home of a Friend of Léger, Paris,
    1985, *132*
  MoMA, December 1985, 1985, *134*
Lawson, Thomas
  Christminster, 1984, *11*

Leather vest, 1969–72, *154*
Leatherdale, Marcus, *29*
Le Journal des dames et des modes, *80*
Les Modes, *126*
Levine, Sherrie
    Untitled, 1984, *8*
Lowit, Roxanne, *55, 69, 81, 107*

Mme Poiret Wearing "La Faune,"
    1919, *130*
Mlle Charlotte du Val d'Ognes, c. 1810, *90*
Manet, Edouard
    The Bar at the Folies-Bergère,
        1881–82, *14*
    Le Déjeuner sur l'herbe, 1862–63, *14*
Man Ray, *130*
Man's ensemble, c. 1785, *82*
Mantegna, Andrea
    Ludovico III Gonzaga among His
        Relatives, 1471–74, *46*
Manuscripts
    The Emperor John Cantacuzenus,
        14th century, *30*
    Les Quatre Fils Aymon: Marriage of
        Renaud de Montauban and Clarisse,
        c. 1450, *42*
Mariani, Carlo Maria
    Il mano ubbidisce all'intelletto, 1983, *92*
Marineau, Guy, *67*
Mary Fitton, c. 1595, *56*
Mary Hill (Mrs. Mackwilliam),
    c. 1585–90, *52*
Matsuda, *see* Matsuda, Mitsuhiro
Matsuda, Mitsuhiro
    Suit, 1989, *121*
McCoy, Ann
    Barque with Lion Goddess III, 1985, *18*
McDermott, David, and Peter McGough
    1917, 1988, *13*
McFadden, Mary
    Evening gown, 1986, *29*
Miyake, Issey
    Jacket and tights, 1989, *1, 87*
    Sweater dress, 1988–89, *45*
Mosaic
    Consecration of San Vitale,
        6th century, *28*
Moschino, Franco
    Evening dress, 1989, *135*
    Man's hippie ensemble, 1988, *153*
    Napoleonic cavalry ensemble,
        1988–89, *93*
    Pants ensemble, 1988–89, *59*
    Pinwheel suit, 1988, *6, 145*
Mummy, Egyptian, *18*

Nagy, Peter
    Belief in Style, 1988, *72*
Nelson, Joan
    Untitled (162), 1987, *66*
    Untitled (180), 1988, *70*

Newman, Barnett
    Who's Afraid of Red, Yellow, and Blue II,
        1967, *13*

Oil flask, Athenian, 5th century B.C., *20*
Oliver, Isaac
    Portrait of an Unknown Man,
        16th century, *54*
Ororbia Master
    Flagellation of Christ, c. 1530, *40*

Pages, Jean
    Fashion illustration, 1931, *136*
Paulin, Guy
    Day dress, 1988, *79, 156*
Pauquet, H.
    Dance, 1763, *72*
Peace medallion, c. 1970, *152*
Poirier, Anne and Patrick
    Pegasus, 1984, *22*
Pollaiuolo, Piero and Antonio
    Galeazzo Maria Sforza, c. 1470–76, *36*
Price, Anthony
    Evening dress, 1986, *111*

Quilted petticoat, 18th century, *76*

Rabanne, Paco
    Minidress, c. 1968, *146*
Reedspear Tournament at Valladolid,
    1506, *36*
Rhodes, Zandra
    Evening gown, 1981, *57*
Roehm, Carolyne
    Minidress, 1988, *149*
Roversi, Paolo, *91*

Saalburg, Leslie L.
    Fashion plate, 1922, *132*
Saari, Peter
    Untitled, 1984, *11*
    Untitled, 1985, *26*
Saint Laurent, Yves
    Wedding gown, 1986, *101*
Santerre, Jean-Baptiste
    Marie Adelaide Savoie, Duchess of
        Burgundy, 1709, *64*
Scharf, Kenny
    Felix on a Pedestal, 1982, *154*
Schwab, Pierre, *153*
Seidner, David, *47, 51, 82*
Sheehan, Maura
    The Bearded Lady, 1985, *20*
    Elapsed Time, 1986–87, *24*
Sirko, Cindy, *19, 23*
Sitbon, Martine
    Evening pants ensemble, 1988, *151*
    Shirts, 1988–89, *frontispiece, 95*
Skrebneski, Victor, *113*
Stirling, James, and Michael Wilford
    Neue Staatsgalerie, Stuttgart,
        1977–84, *7*

Stone, Sly, *150*
Sturtevant, Elaine
    Lichtenstein Study for Frightened Girl,
        1988, *148*
Sullivan, Bill
    Bench, 1988, *24*

Taaffe, Philip
    We Are Not Afraid, 1985, *13*
Tanagra statuette, 3rd century B.C., *22*
Tansey, Mark
    Source of the Loue, 1988, *15*
    Triumph over Mastery, 1987, *46*
Tapestry
    Catherine de Médicis, 16th century, *50*
Thomass, Chantal
    Evening pants ensemble, 1989–90, *83*
Tigerman, Stanley
    Pediment chair, 1982, *20*
T-shirt, tie-dyed, 1969–72, *154*
Tissot, James
    Too Early, 1873, *104*

Vallhonrat, *139, 141, 143*
van Dyke, Anthony
    The Abbe Scalia, 1634–35, *60*
Varty, Keith, and Alan Cleaver
    Winter suit, 1988–89, *115*
Venturi, Robert
    Queen Anne chair, 1984, *8*
Vernet, Carle
    Parisian Incroyable, c. 1790–1800, *86*
Vodofsky, Marc, *65, 73*

Watson, Albert, *151*
Watteau, Antoine
    French Comedians, c. 1720–21, *70*
    Pierrot, or Gilles, c. 1718–19, *66*
    The Shop Sign, or *Gersaint's Shop Sign*,
        c. 1720, *68*
    Standing Woman Seen from Behind,
        c. 1715, *9*
Weiditz, Christoph
    Das Trachtenbuch, 1529, *38*
Wiegel, Hans
    Das Trachtenbuch: Habitus, 1577, *48*
Women's Auxiliary Corps, 1918, *128*

Yamamoto, Yohji
    Evening dress, 1988–89, *109*